THE
BLESSING
OF
ABRAHAM
IS
MINE

KOLAWOLE
ANTHONY

SOPHOS
SB
BOOKS

THE BLESSING OF ABRAHAM IS MINE
Secrets to the Life of Continuous Provision
Copyright © 2023 by Kolawole Anthony

Published by
Sophos Books
163 Warbank Crescent
Croydon
CR0 0AZ

Unless otherwise indicated, scripture quotations are from the New King James Version of the Bible, copyright © 1982 by Thomas Nelson Inc. All emphasis within Scripture quotations are the author's own.

ISBN 978-1-905669-81-3

Cover design by *Icon Media*
Printed in the United Kingdom

Contents

1

GOD'S WILL

God's desire for us as believers is that we prosper and be in health as our soul prospers.

> *"Beloved, I wish above all things that thou mayest prosper and be in health, even as thy soul prospereth."* **III John 1:2 KJV**

God sent His Son Jesus Christ to die for us so that we can be Blessed. So, if we are not blessed and prosperous, we are not making God happy.

> *"Christ has redeemed us from the curse of the law, having become a curse for us (for it is written, "Cursed is everyone who*

> *hangs on a tree"), that the blessing of*
> *Abraham might come upon the Gentiles in*
> *Christ Jesus, that we might receive the*
> *promise of the Spirit through faith."*
> **Galatians 3:13-14 KJV**

Some people are of the opinion that a believer in Christ ought to be poor. In their mind, poverty will ensure humility and meekness. Well, this is totally unscriptural and ungodly. God's will for all His children is prosperity. When you study God's Word, you will not find anyone associated with God was held captive by poverty. Everyone who related closely with God operated in financial dominion.

> *"He also brought them out with silver*
> *and gold, And there was none feeble*
> *among His tribes."* **Psalm 105:37**
> **NKJV**

The Bible is littered with stories that show God's will concerning poverty, prosperity, and financial dominion. One that has been a tremendous blessing to me is the story of the woman whose husband, a son of the prophet, did not have the revelation of financial dominion. He died and left his wife and kids in serious debt.

First point to note is that living a life of poverty and dying in debt is not God's will for His children. Rather, He wants us to leave an inheritance for our children and grandchildren.

> *"If you obey God, you will have something to leave your grandchildren. If you don't obey God, those who live right will get what you leave."* **Proverbs 13:22 CEV**

So, this woman was in a very bad situation. She was in debt and risked losing her kids to the debt collectors. Unlike her husband, she knew that God was not in favour of poverty. She also knew that obedience was key for financial dominion. So, she went after God's servant, Elisha. She knew the answer to her situation was in God.

> *"A certain woman of the wives of the sons of the prophets cried out to Elisha, saying, "Your servant my husband is dead, and you know that your servant feared the*

Lord. And the creditor is coming to take my two sons to be his slaves."

So, Elisha said to her, "What shall I do for you? Tell me, what do you have in the house?" And she said, "Your maidservant has nothing in the house but a jar of oil."

Then he said, "Go, borrow vessels from everywhere, from all your neighbours empty vessels; do not gather just a few. And when you have come in, you shall shut the door behind you and your sons; then pour it into all those vessels, and set aside the full ones."

So, she went from him and shut the door behind her and her sons, who brought the vessels to her; and she poured it out. Now it came to pass, when the vessels were full, that she said to her son, "Bring me another vessel."

And he said to her, "There is not another vessel." So, the oil ceased. Then she came and told the man of God. And he said, "Go, sell the oil and pay your debt; and you and your sons live on the rest."

2 Kings 4:1-7 NKJV

God, through the Prophet, gave her an instruction to borrow as many vessels as she can from her neighbours, close the door behind her, and pour out the oil in the tiny jar into the borrowed vessels. She obeyed God's instruction even though it was illogical. How do you pour a tiny bit of oil into lots of bigger vessels? It simply did not make sense!

A lot of people have lost out on their financial breakthrough because God's instruction to them did not make sense. It did not sit well with their PhD in Economics and Management. But this woman obeyed God's seemingly nonsensical instruction and in no time at all, she was debt free and enjoyed financial dominion. Indeed, poverty is a curse and God's will for us is dominion over poverty. That is why Jesus sacrificed His body on the cross to redeem us and give us Grace to walk in the Blessings of Abraham.

PERSONAL NOTES

_____

_____

_____

_____

_____

_____

_____

_____

_____

_____

_____

_____

_____

_____

_____

_____

_____

_____

_____

_____

_____

_____

_____

_____

_____

_____

_____

_____

_____

_____

_____

_____

_____

_____

_____

_____

_____

_____

_____

_____

_____

_____

_____

_____

_____

_____

2

THE BLESSING OF ABRAHAM

God desires that we should be blessed like Abraham was. The question is what does that look like? It is always important to have visual images because as human beings, we can only experience what we are able to imagine. We can only go as far as we can see.

> *"After Lot had gone, the LORD said to Abram, "Look as far as you can see in every direction—north and south, east and west. I am giving all this land, as far as you can see, to you and your descendants as a permanent possession. And I will give you so many descendants*

*that, like the dust of the earth, they cannot
be counted! Go and walk through the land
in every direction, for I am giving it to
you."* **Genesis 13:14-17 NLT**

The truth is, you cannot have faith for what you
cannot see. So, until we are able to build an image
of what Abraham's blessing look like, confessing
that Abraham's blessing belong to us will simply
be a waste of time and energy. In the walk of the
Spirit, your imagination is very important. When
God instructed Abraham to look North, South,
East, and West, and to walk through the land in
every direction, He wasn't asking him to do so
physically; He instructed him to engage his
imagination.

God was teaching Abraham the fundamentals
of creating your world by faith. Remember the
Tower of Babel. The people on the earth at the time
understood the power of agreement and
imagination as it relates to creation. They came
into agreement in their imagination and God
acknowledged that they had tapped into a power
source that was limitless.

*"And the LORD said, Behold, the people
is one, and they have all one language;
and this they begin to do: and now
nothing will be restrained from them,
which they have imagined to do."*
Genesis 11:6 KJV

It is my hope that once you can see what
Abraham's blessing looks like, you will release
your faith to believe for the same experience in
your life. Paul, in his letter to the Ephesians,
reveals that God is able to do much more than we
can imagine.

*"Now to him who is able to do
immeasurably more than all we ask or
imagine, according to his power that is at
work within us."* **Ephesians 3:20 NIV**

Divine Favour

Abraham's blessing confers on the believer
God's divine favour. In the process of obedience
(and that's very important), Abraham moved
from Harran to Shechem. However, because of the

famine in the land, he moved to Egypt. On arrival in Egypt, he realised that there was a big problem. the Egyptians liked pretty women and his wife Sarah was stunning. As expected, the men in Egypt noticed Sarah was 'hot like fire' and decided she would be a fantastic addition to their king, Pharaoh's harem.

> *"Now there was a famine in the land, and Abram went down to Egypt to dwell there, for the famine was severe in the land. And it came to pass, when he was close to entering Egypt, that he said to Sarai his wife, "Indeed I know that you are a woman of beautiful countenance. Therefore, it will happen, when the Egyptians see you, that they will say, 'This is his wife'; and they will kill me, but they will let you live. Please say you are my sister, that it may be well with me for your sake, and that I may live because of you."* **Genesis 12:10-13 NKJV**

You would have expected Abraham to stand up for his wife and put his life on the line. After all, he was a man of God. Unfortunately, Abraham was scared like we all can be and decided to lie to the Egyptians, or tell them a half truth, which is actually still a lie. His darling wife, Sarah was taken from him (with his consent) and she lived in Pharaohs house. She basically became Pharaoh's wife.

The obvious example of divine favour from this story is that Pharaoh treated Abraham well because of his wife Sarah.

> "And he entreated Abram well for her sake: and he had sheep, and oxen, and he asses, and menservants, and maidservants, and she asses, and camels." **Genesis 12:16 KJV**

But we miss out on a deeper manifestation of God's favour which is that God protected Sarah, Abraham's wife, from being defiled by the Pharaoh. Sarah was not Pharaoh's wife for a week, no. She was in his house for quite a while, and she probably was one of the most beautiful women the Pharaoh had in his house. Imagine if Pharaoh were anything like king David or king Solomon! Without the favour of God, it wouldn't have taken more than a night for Pharaoh to defile her. Her body, her sanity, her dignity was protected because of God's divine favour.

> *"But the LORD sent terrible plagues upon Pharaoh and his household because of Sarai, Abram's wife. So, Pharaoh summoned Abram and accused him sharply. "What have you done to me?" he demanded. "Why didn't you tell me she was your wife? Why did you say, 'She is my sister,' and allow me to take her as my wife? Now then, here is your wife. Take her and get out of here!"* **Genesis 12:17-19 NLT**

Divine favour can be defined as being preferred, liked, approved, supported, and regarded over others by God, especially in a way that's seems unfair. This is a characteristic of the blessing of Abraham. After it became obvious that Abraham had not been too forthright about his relationship with Sarah, Pharaoh could have imprisoned or beheaded, or make him return all he had received for Sarah. But because of divine favour, he ordered that Abraham be sent away unharmed with all he had given him.

*"And Abram went up out of Egypt, he,
and his wife, and all that he had, and Lot
with him, into the south. And Abram was
very rich in cattle, in silver, and in gold"*

My prayer for every Believer in Jesus Christ is
that you will desire to experience the favour that
Abraham enjoyed in Jesus' name.

Healing

The Blessing of Abraham guarantees sound
health, healing, and longevity. Abraham finally
obeyed God at age 75. Some preachers have
taught that immediately God instructed Abraham
to leave his family, he packed his bags and left.
That couldn't be further from the truth. Genesis
12:1 says:

*"Now the LORD had said unto Abram,
Get thee out of thy country, and from thy
kindred, and from thy father's house,
unto a land that I will shew thee:"*

Notice that God had told Abraham a while ago

to leave his father's house ("the Lord *had said*"). But he did not obey for reasons best known to him. When he was 75 years old, he decided it was time to do what God had instructed him to do. In the place of obedience, Abraham's blessing released God's quickening (healing), health, and longevity.

I don't know exactly when Abraham married Sarah, but I would guess (based on the culture back in those days when people generally got married very early) perhaps at 25 years of age. If that was the case, it means at 75, he would have been married to Sarah for nearly 50 years without having kids. They were both officially barren.

Now, the Lord had said to Abraham he would be the Father of many nations (Genesis 12:2), and Abraham believed. But I am not sure Sarah shared in Abraham's enthusiasm because she must have known Abraham was no longer able to perform in bed. He could have been suffering from impotency or erectile dysfunction or both (which could have informed Abraham's decision to lie that Sarah was not his wife. It's not written in scripture, so I do not know for sure. It is just a thought).

Anyway, I think Sarah was getting a bit frustrated around the house, so she decided to carry out an experiment to silence Abraham and bring him back to his senses. She decided to give Hagar, a young Egyptian maid, to Abraham to sleep with at the age of 84.

"Now Sarai, Abram's wife, had borne him no children. But she had an Egyptian slave named Hagar; so she said to Abram, The Lord has kept me from having children. Go, sleep with my slave; perhaps I can build a family through her.

Abram agreed to what Sarai said. So, after Abram had been living in Canaan ten years, Sarai his wife took her Egyptian slave Hagar and gave her to her husband to be his wife. He slept with Hagar, and she conceived.

When she knew she was pregnant, she began to despise her mistress. Then Sarai said to Abram, "You are responsible for the wrong I am suffering. I put my slave in your arms, and now that she knows she is pregnant, she despises me. May the Lord judge between you and me."

Your slave is in your hands," Abram

> *said. "Do with her whatever you think*
> *best." Then Sarai mistreated Hagar; so*
> *she fled from her."* **Genesis 16:1-6 NIV**

In that part of the world, it was culturally acceptable for a woman to raise children through her maid. When Rachel, Jacob's wife, was challenged as Sarah was, she gave her maid, Bilhah, to her husband as a wife. And when Leah, her sister, thought she was being outwitted, she gave her maid, Zilphah, to her husband as well.

> *"When Rachel saw that she was not*
> *bearing Jacob any children, she became*
> *jealous of her sister. So, she said to Jacob,*
> *"Give me children, or I'll die!"*
>
> *Jacob became angry with her and said,*
> *"Am I in the place of God, who has kept*
> *you from having children?"*
>
> *Then she said, "Here is Bilhah, my*
> *servant. Sleep with her so that she can*
> *bear children for me and I too can build a*
> *family through her."*
>
> *So, she gave him her servant Bilhah as a*
> *wife. Jacob slept with her, and she became*

pregnant and bore him a son. Then Rachel said, "God has vindicated me; he has listened to my plea and given me a son." Because of this she named him Dan.

Rachel's servant Bilhah conceived again and bore Jacob a second son. Then Rachel said, "I have had a great struggle with my sister, and I have won." So, she named him Naphtali.

When Leah saw that she had stopped having children, she took her servant Zilpah and gave her to Jacob as a wife. Leah's servant Zilpah bore Jacob a son. Then Leah said, "What good fortune!" So, she named him Gad.

Leah's servant Zilpah bore Jacob a second son. Then Leah said, "How happy I am! The women will call me happy." So, she named him Asher." **Genesis 30:1-15 NIV**

But note the difference in reaction when Bilhah and Zilpah became pregnant. Rachel and Leah rejoiced and treated the children as theirs, giving them amazing names - Dan, Naphtali, Gad, and Asher. Why was Rachel and Leah excited and

Sarah unhappy? In my opinion, Rachel and Leah were expecting their husband to do the business, they knew he was a certified 'striker' while Sarah was not expecting her husband to get the job done, she knew he had problems getting it up.

My purpose in forensically analysing the mindset of the players in these stories is not to denigrate Sarah, but to prove that the healing of our bodies is included in the blessing of Abraham. Sarah did not believe Abraham was going to have an erection. She knew her husband was dead sexually. Let's read Romans 4:17 (KJV)

> *"(As it is written, I have made thee a father of many nations,) before him whom he believed, even God, who quickeneth the dead, and calleth those things which be not as though they were."*

Abraham was not brought back to life like Lazarus was and he never prayed for anyone who was dead. When did he experience God as the one who quickeneth the dead? The only instance recorded in scripture where he could have experienced God's quickening power before he was

100years old was when God quickened his dead body and he was able to supernaturally impregnate Hagar the Egyptian. God supernaturally restored his erectile functions and healed him of impotency. Indeed, there is healing power in the blessing of Abraham.

I don't know what Satan has afflicted you with, but I know God is a healer and He is able to quicken the dead. Christ has redeemed us from every curse of the law and in its place we have access to the blessing of Abraham. That blessing is able to heal every sickness and disease, the blessing healed Abraham's dead body. Friends and family may have given up on you; the physicians may have given you a terminal verdict; but you are the next in line for a miracle that will surprise everyone around you in Jesus mighty name.

Sound Health and Longevity

The Blessing of Abraham ensures the healing of our bodies, but healing is for those who are sick and diseased. Our God is also able to maintain the health of those who obey and serve Him. He is able to keep them lively and healthy until they are satisfied with life.

> *"With long life I will satisfy him, And show him My salvation."*
> **Psalm 91:6 NKJV**

We will still get back to Abraham but let's look at Moses' testimony.

> *"Moses was a hundred and twenty years old when he died, yet his eyes were not weak nor his strength gone."* **Genesis 34:7 NIV**

Caleb, at 85, said his strength had not diminished in 45 years. He was still able to fight at the of 85. Incredible!

> *"Now, as you can see, the LORD has kept me alive and well as he promised for all these forty-five years since Moses made this promise — even while Israel wandered in the wilderness. Today I am eighty-five years old. I am as strong now*

*as I was when Moses sent me on that
journey, and I can still travel and fight as
well as I could then. So, give me the hill
country that the LORD promised me."*
Joshua 14:10-12 NLT

The God of Abraham is able to sustain the
health of those that obey and serve Him, and
prosper them like He did His friend Abraham. See
what the prophet Elihu said to Job:

*"If they obey and serve him, they shall
spend their days in prosperity, and their
years in pleasures."* **Job 36:11-12 KJV**

No one can live a pleasurable life in sickness
and disease. God's will for us is a healthy life.

When Joseph presented Jacob to Pharaoh, for
some reason Pharaoh had to ask how old he was. I
think Pharaoh was baffled at the longevity of
Jacob.

*"Then Joseph brought his father Jacob in
and presented him before Pharaoh. After
Jacob blessed Pharaoh, Pharaoh asked
him, "How old are you?"*

And Jacob said to Pharaoh, "The years of my pilgrimage are a hundred and thirty. My years have been few and difficult, and they do not equal the years of the pilgrimage of my fathers." Then Jacob blessed Pharaoh and went out from his presence." **Genesis 47:7-10 NIV**

At 130 years of age, Jacob considered his years as few. He was dissatisfied with his life (we know the story of Jacob how he deceived his older brother to steal his birthright). He felt he had not lived the quality and length of life his dad and grandad lived. His father, Isaac, was 180 years old when he died. What an awesome God.

"Then Jacob came to his father Isaac at Mamre, or Kirjath Arba (that is, Hebron), where Abraham and Isaac had dwelt. Now the days of Isaac were one hundred and eighty years. So, Isaac breathed his last and died, and was gathered to his people, being old and full of days. And his sons Esau and Jacob buried him." **Genesis 35:27-29 NKJV**

Abraham's wife, Sarah, lived to 127 years of age. She gave birth to Isaac at the age of 90 when Abraham was 100 years old.

> *"Then Abraham fell on his face and laughed, and said in his heart, "Shall a child be born to a man who is one hundred years old? And shall Sarah, who is ninety years old, bear a child?" And Abraham said to God, "Oh, that Ishmael might live before You!"* **Genesis 17:17-18 NKJV**

At age of 100, Abraham considered himself old and unable to have another child, but God again visited Abraham and quickened his body. He also visited Sarah and terminated her barrenness. God then went further and renewed Abraham's youth.

After the death of Sarah, Abraham's youth was so renewed that he married another woman, Keturah. His sexual dysfunction was history and he had loads of kids through Keturah.

> *"Abraham again took a wife, and her name was Keturah. And she bore him Zimran, Jokshan, Medan, Midian,*

> *Ishbak, and Shuah. Jokshan begot Sheba*
> *and Dedan. And the sons of Dedan were*
> *Asshurim, Letushim, and Leummim.*
> *And the sons of Midian were Ephah,*
> *Epher, Hanoch, Abidah, and Eldaah. All*
> *these were the children of Keturah."*
> **Genesis 25:1-4 NKJV**

Abraham did not just have another wife, he was so restored he had several concubines and had kids from them. What a God!

> *"And Abraham gave all that he had to*
> *Isaac. But Abraham gave gifts to the sons*
> *of the concubines which Abraham had;*
> *and while he was still living he sent them*
> *eastward, away from Isaac his son, to the*
> *country of the east"* **Genesis 25:5**
> **NKJV**

This revelation should be enough for any man reading this book to step out of every erectile dysfunction and any form of impotence. I also believe by the experience of Sarah, any woman reading this book, who is confirmed barren, should receive total deliverance in the mighty name of Jesus. You cannot be walking in the blessings of Abraham and remain impotent or barren. If you do what Abraham did, you will experience what he experienced in Jesus name.

Abraham went on to live till he was 175 years. Evidently, he lived a fantastic, vibrant, productive, and fulfilled life. This is the lot of every believer walking in the blessings of Abraham.

> *"Abraham lived a total of 175 years. And at a ripe old age he breathed his last and died, old and contented, and was gathered to his people."* **Genesis 25:8 KJV**

A Man of Influence

The blessing of Abraham makes a believer an influential personality amongst family, friends, neighbours, and the community. Prior to stepping out in obedience to God, Abraham was just another man living with his dad. But his story began to change after he decided to obey God. He became a reference point in his family.

Lot, Abraham's nephew, was blessed because of his uncle. They were doing alright financially when they left Haran. But in just a few years, their possessions were so great they could not dwell together. That is the power of God.

> *"Lot also, who went with Abram, had flocks and herds and tents. Now the land was not able to support them, that they might dwell together, for their possessions were so great that they could not dwell together"* **Genesis 13:5-6 NKJV**

Abraham was not just influential in his family; he was also a force to reckon with in the community. His influence was in full display during the battle of the kings, at the Valley of Shaveh, where he and his private army defeated King Chedorlaomer and the three kings that were with him.

> *"And the vale of Siddim was full of slimepits; and the kings of Sodom and Gomorrah fled, and fell there; and they that remained fled to the mountain. And they took all the goods of Sodom and Gomorrah, and all their victuals, and went their way. And they took Lot, Abram's*

brother's son, who dwelt in Sodom, and his goods, and departed.

And there came one that had escaped, and told Abram the Hebrew; for he dwelt in the plain of Mamre the Amorite, brother of Eshcol, and brother of Aner: and these were confederate with Abram. And when Abram heard that his brother was taken captive, he armed his trained servants, born in his own house, three hundred and eighteen, and pursued them unto Dan. And he divided himself against them, he and his servants, by night, and smote them, and pursued them unto Hobah, which is on the left hand of Damascus. And he brought back all the goods, and also brought again his brother Lot, and his goods, and the women also, and the people." **Genesis 14:10-16 KJV**

King Chedorlaomer was a dominant king in that part of the world at the time and for 12 years, all the other kings paid some form of taxes to him. The war that engulfed Lot, Abraham's nephew, was because of the refusal of some of the kings to pay taxes to King Chedorlaomer (Genesis 14:1-

10). For Abraham to defeat these armies was a very loud statement to all the nations in the region. It basically made Abraham the dominant military force in the region.

Aside from being influential militarily, Abraham was a force to reckon with financially. It costs a lot of money to have a private army. Being wealthy is essential for influence. Some believers are of the opinion that once they are wise and heavenly bound they're good to go – not quite so. King Solomon told the story of a poor wise man that saved a small town by his wisdom, but because he was poor, his influence was short lived.

> *"There was a small town with only a few people, and a great king came with his army and besieged it. A poor, wise man knew how to save the town, and so it was rescued. But afterward no one thought to thank him. So even though wisdom is better than strength, those who are wise will be despised if they are poor. What they say will not be appreciated for long."*
> **Ecclesiastes 9:14-16 NLT**

Abraham was not a poor man. His servant described Abraham's wealth when he was looking for a wife for Isaac:

> *"And the LORD has greatly blessed my master; he has become a wealthy man. The LORD has given him flocks of sheep and goats, herds of cattle, a fortune in silver and gold, and many male and female servants and camels and donkeys."*
> **Genesis 24:35 NLT**

The blessing of Abraham is a guarantee that the believer would live a life of financial abundance, a life of more than enough, just like Abraham did. My prayer is that your family, friends, and community would call you blessed, and that God will enlarge your coast and make you a delightsome land in Jesus mighty name.

These are some of the attributes that make up the blessing of Abraham, so Galatians 3:13 says Christ has redeemed us from sin that we who accept Him as Lord and Saviour can walk in these attributes here on the earth. So how do we achieve these?

PERSONAL NOTES

_____

_____

_____

_____

_____

_____

_____

_____

_____

_____

_____

_____

_____

_____

_____

_____

_____

_____

_____

_____

_____

_____

_____

_____

_____

_____

_____

_____

_____

_____

_____

_____

_____

_____

_____

_____

_____

_____

_____

_____

_____

_____

_____

3

KEYS TO ABRAHAM'S BLESSING

How did Abraham become so Blessed?

Obedience

The first and most important key to walking in the blessing of Abraham as a believer is obedience.

> *"If you are willing and obedient, You shall eat the good of the land; But if you refuse and rebel, You shall be devoured by the sword"; For the mouth of the Lord has spoken."* **Isaiah 1:19-20 NKJV**

Abraham obeyed God's instruction to leave his family and follow God unto an unknown location. It took him a while to obey (like many of us) and while he was in disobedience, he was a nobody. But when he eventually decided to obey God (at 75 years of age), everything changed and he became a super success.

> *"Now the Lord had said unto Abram, Get thee out of thy country, and from thy kindred, and from thy father's house, unto a land that I will shew thee:*
> *And I will make of thee a great nation, and I will bless thee, and make thy name great; and thou shalt be a blessing:*
> *And I will bless them that bless thee, and curse him that curseth thee: and in thee shall all families of the earth be blessed."*
> **Genesis 12:1-3 KJV**

Isaac's story of the blessing also started with obedience:

> *"And there was a famine in the land, beside the first famine that was in the days of Abraham. And Isaac went unto*

Abimelech king of the Philistines unto Gerar.

And the LORD appeared unto him, and said, Go not down into Egypt; dwell in the land which I shall tell thee of: Sojourn in this land, and I will be with thee, and will bless thee; for unto thee, and unto thy seed, I will give all these countries, and I will perform the oath which I sware unto Abraham thy father; And I will make thy seed to multiply as the stars of heaven, and will give unto thy seed all these countries; and in thy seed shall all the nations of the earth be blessed; Because that Abraham obeyed my voice, and kept my charge, my commandments, my statutes, and my laws. And Isaac dwelt in Gerar"

Genesis 26:1-6 KJV

I love the scripture in Job 36:11-12 [NKJV]:

"If they obey and serve Him, they shall spend their days in prosperity, and their years in pleasures.

> *But if they do not obey, they shall perish*
> *by the sword, and they shall die without*
> *knowledge."*

Obedience is such an important key to experiencing the blessings of Abraham, and in my opinion, it is foundational. Without obedience, any attempt to step into Kingdom prosperity will be futile. In fact, disobedience can be very costly for a child of God. Not only will The Blessing of Abraham be elusive, but it could also result in the believer dying before their time.

Job 36:13-14 states:

> *"But the hypocrites in heart store up*
> *wrath; they do not cry for help when he*
> *binds them.*
> *They die in youth, and their life ends*
> *among the perverted persons."*

This will not be your portion. So, make a determination from today to always choose obedience.

As a born again believer you are a bona fide citizen of Heaven. You must always remember you are no longer just an earthling; you are now a Heavenlian.

The scripture says in 2 Corinthians 5:17-18:
"Therefore, if anyone is in Christ, he is a new creation; old things have passed away; behold, all things have become new. Now all things are of God, who has reconciled us to Himself through Jesus Christ, and has given us the ministry of reconciliation."

Not only are you a citizen of Heaven, you are also now on assignment to bring reconciliation between your community and God as an ambassador of the kingdom of heaven.

"Now then, we are ambassadors for Christ, as though God were pleading through us: we implore you on Christ's behalf, be reconciled to God." **2 Corinthians 5:20**

Before you could become an ambassador of heaven, Jesus Christ redeemed you with His precious blood.

1 Corinthians 6:10 says:

> *"For you were bought at a price; therefore glorify God in your body and in your spirit, which are God's."*

and Colossians 1:13 (BSB) reads:

> *"He has rescued us from the dominion of darkness and brought us into the kingdom of His beloved Son, in whom we have redemption, the forgiveness of sins."*

In Summary, before you got born again, you were a citizen of the kingdom of darkness and under Satan's dominion. But Jesus paid the price with His flesh and blood (Colossians 1:19-22) to deliver you from the dominion of darkness and transfer you into the kingdom of heaven.

You no longer belong to yourself; you now belong to Jesus, and are now reconciled back to God. By this miraculous deliverance, you can now fulfil the purpose for which you have been created. Fortunately, the blueprint of your life in its entirety is only known to God.

"But as it is written: "Eye has not seen, nor ear heard, Nor have entered into the heart of man The things which God has prepared for those who love Him." **1 Corinthians 2:9**

Your purpose as an Ambassador is to carry out that original destiny that God created you to fulfil to his glory and to the advancement of His kingdom. You cannot do that except you walk with the Holy Spirit in obedience just like Abraham and Isaac did.

Isaiah 48:17 reads:

"Thus says the LORD, your Redeemer, The Holy One of Israel: "I am the LORD your God, Who teaches you to profit, Who leads you by the way you should go."

and John 16:13 reads:

"However, when He, the Spirit of truth, has come, He will guide you into all truth; for He will not speak on His own authority, but whatever He hears He will

speak; and He will tell you things to come."

The Holy Spirit is called Wisdom in the book of Proverbs. Solomon revealed the importance of walking in obedience to God in Proverbs 8:12-21:

I wisdom dwell with prudence, and find out knowledge of witty inventions.

The fear of the LORD is to hate evil: pride, and arrogancy, and the evil way, and the froward mouth, do I hate.

Counsel is mine, and sound wisdom: I am understanding; I have strength.

By me kings reign, and princes decree justice.

By me princes rule, and nobles, even all the judges of the earth.

I love them that love me; and those that seek me early shall find me.

Riches and honour are with me; yea, durable riches and righteousness.

My fruit is better than gold, yea, than fine gold; and my revenue than choice silver.

I lead in the way of righteousness, in the midst of the paths of judgment:

> *That I may cause those that love me to inherit substance; and I will fill their treasures*

The only way we can walk in the blessing of Abraham is if we are committed to living as ambassadors for Christ, and that can only be by walking in obedience to the voice and prompting of the Holy Spirit on a day-to-day basis. There is no other way to prosper in the Kingdom of God.

Tithing

The second and very important key to walking in the blessing of Abraham is in understanding the mystery of tithing.

> *"Then Melchizedek king of Salem brought out bread and wine; he was the priest of God Most High. And he blessed him and said: "Blessed be Abram of God Most High, Possessor of heaven and earth; And blessed be God Most High, Who has delivered your enemies into your hand." And he gave him a tithe of all."* **Genesis 14:18-20 NKJV**

There is a lot of debate in the Church today about tithing. Some people think tithing is part of the old covenant and should not be practised in the new. Some people say it is a con being deployed by ministers to defraud Church members. There is a lot of negativities surrounding tithing and I can totally understand why. A lot of believers have paid their tithes faithfully for a long time and they have not seen the promises associated with tithing in their lives. On the other hand, they are seeing Pastors getting wealthy, buying very expensive things and living very ostentatious lives. So yes! I can understand why many believers are frustrated with paying tithes.

Firstly, tithing is a not new or an Old Testament practice; it is an eternal mystery instituted by the Almighty God for the blessing of mankind. In fact, tithing was instituted in the Garden of Eden when God created Adam and Eve.

> *"Then the Lord God took the man and put him in the garden of Eden to tend and keep it. And the Lord God commanded the man, saying, "Of every tree of the garden you may freely eat; but of the tree of the knowledge of good and evil you shall not*

eat, for in the day that you eat of it you shall surely die." **Genesis 2:15-17 NKJV**

So, God gave Adam and Eve all the trees of the garden to eat, but he instructed them not to eat the fruit of one of the trees. Isn't that what the tithe is? God is the one that gives us everything that we have:

> *"Thou openest thine hand, and satisfiest the desire of every living thing."*
> **Psalm 145:16**

And he says out of everything I have given you, if you really believe I am the one that has given you all that you have: the job, the business breakthrough, that amazing idea etc. I want you to set aside a tenth of the profit or the increase and worship me with it.

Not the bit you can do without like Cain brought to the Lord and it was rejected but the best bit like Abel sacrificed to The Lord and was accepted.

> *"So, in the course of time, Cain brought some of the fruit of the soil as an offering to the LORD, while Abel brought the best portions of the firstborn of his flock.*
>
> *And the LORD looked with favour on Abel and his offering, but He had no regard for Cain and his offering. So, Cain became very angry, and his countenance fell.*
>
> *"Why are you angry," said the LORD to Cain, "and why has your countenance fallen? If you do what is right, will you not be accepted? But if you refuse to do what is right, sin is crouching at your door; it desires you, but you must master it."* **Genesis 4:3-7 BSB**

The tithe is not a Christian practice, and it was not instituted by Moses. The tithe had been from the beginning. Have you ever wondered who taught Abraham to pay tithes? How did Jacob learn to pay his tithes to the Lord? The tithe has been from the beginning and it was practised by everyone that believed, feared and respected God. It is not an Old Testament practice, and cannot be invalidated by the new testament. The Tithe is an eternal mystery put in place by God for mankind to walk in the blessing - to be fruitful, multiply, replenish the earth, subdue the earth and walk in dominion.

And Isaac Sowed In That Land

The third key to walking in the blessing of Abraham is to take advantage of opportunities God brings your way using your God-given talents.

> *"Then Isaac sowed in that land, and reaped in the same year a hundredfold; and the Lord blessed him. The man began to prosper, and continued prospering until he became very prosperous; for he had possess ions of flocks and possessions of herds and a great number of servants. So the Philistines envied him."* **Genesis 26:12-14 NKJV**

Isaac inherited all of Abraham's possessions - the servants, herds of cattle, the flocks of sheep and goats, the fortune in silver and gold and the camels and donkeys. But there was a famine and Isaac was contemplating moving to Egypt like everyone else. God showed up and instructed him not to move to Egypt but rather stay in Gerar despite the famine.

Isaac obeyed and decided to sow in Gerar. What does it mean for Isaac to sow in the land? It means that Isaac invested in Gerar. He perhaps bought the businesses of his competitors who had decided to move to Egypt because of the famine. He must have invested in more ranches and in more staff and built more infrastructure despite the fact that there was a famine, simply because God instructed him not to move to Egypt but rather to stay put in Gerar.

The Bible says in doing these things, his business became successful year on year until he became a force to reckon with in the land of the Philistines.

> *"Then Abimelech went to him from Gerar, and Ahuzzath one of his friends, and Phichol the chief captain of his army. And Isaac said unto them, Wherefore come ye to me, seeing ye hate me, and have*

sent me away from you? And they said, We saw certainly that the LORD was with thee: and we said, Let there be now an oath betwixt us, even betwixt us and thee, and let us make a covenant with thee; That thou wilt do us no hurt, as we have not touched thee, and as we have done unto thee nothing but good, and have sent thee away in peace: thou art now the blessed of the LORD." **Genesis 26:26-29 KJV**

For us to walk in the blessing of Abraham, we need to invest in the opportunities that God leads us into - we need to sow in the land. What idea has God placed in your heart? What talents God has given to you? Invest in your talents and in your God-given ideas. Don't be lazy. Spend quality time developing yourself and your business. As you do this, God will increase you a hundredfold just like He did Isaac; you will prosper and continue prospering until you become very prosperous.

Kingdom Mindedness

The fourth key to walking in the blessing of Abraham is to commit to serving God with your

life and your resources. One of my favourite
scriptures is Matthew 6:33 [KJV]:

> *"But seek ye first the kingdom of God,*
> *and his righteousness; and all these things*
> *shall be added unto you."*

To walk in the blessing of Abraham, you need to
make the advancement of God's Kingdom your
number one priority. You cannot be a 'me, myself
and I' kind of person and expect the super
abundance of God. It doesn't quite work like that.
God has a plan and purpose for your life as it
relates to His Kingdom, and committing your
resources to the fulfillment of His purpose is key.
Supporting ministries that you know are truly and
genuinely engaged in the advancement of the
Kingdom of God is also vital.

Haggai 1: 2-11 [BSB] explains this very clearly.

> *"This is what the LORD of Hosts says:*
> *"These people say, 'The time has not yet*
> *come to rebuild the house of the LORD.'"*
> *Then the word of the LORD came through*
> *Haggai the prophet, saying: "Is it a time*

for you yourselves to live in your panelled houses, while this house lies in ruins?" Now this is what the LORD of Hosts says: "Consider carefully your ways.

You have planted much but harvested little. You eat but never have enough. You drink but never have your fill. You put on clothes but never get warm. You earn wages to put into a bag pierced through."

This is what the LORD of Hosts says: "Consider carefully your ways.

Go up into the hills, bring down lumber, and build the house, so that I may take pleasure in it and be glorified, says the LORD.

You expected much, but behold, it amounted to little. And what you brought home, I blew away.

Why? declares the LORD of Hosts.

Because My house still lies in ruins, while each of you is busy with his own house. Therefore, on account of you the heavens have withheld their dew and the earth has withheld its crops. I have summoned a drought on the fields and on the mountains, on the grain, new wine, and oil, and on whatever the ground yields, on man and beast, and on all the labour of your hands."

PERSONAL NOTES

_____

_____

_____

_____

_____

_____

_____

_____

_____

_____

_____

_____

_____

_____

_____

_____

_____

_____

_____

_____

_____

_____

_____

_____

_____

_____

_____

_____

_____

_____

_____

_____

_____

_____

_____

_____

_____

_____

_____

_____

_____

_____

_____

_____

_____

_____

_____

_____

_____

_____

_____

_____

_____

_____

_____

_____

_____

_____

_____

_____

_____

_____

_____

_____

_____

_____

4

GIVING AND RECEIVING

We hear so much about giving and receiving in Church today. When it is time to take the offerings in Church, these scriptures are often read to us:

> *"Give and it shall be given unto you; good measure, pressed down, and shaken together, and running over, shall men give into your bosom. For with the same measure that ye mete withal it shall be measured to you again."* **Luke 6:38 KJV**

> *"So Jesus answered and said, "Assuredly, I say to you, there is no one who has left house or brothers or sisters or father or*

mother or wife or children or lands, for My sake and the gospel's, who shall not receive a hundredfold now in this time – houses and brothers and sisters and mothers and children and lands, with persecutions and in the age to come, eternal life." **Mark 10:29 KJV**

Now, many Christians have given and continue to give, but they wonder why they are not receiving a good in return. They do not receive anything close to the promised hundredfold. In fact, some believers would be happy if God can just give them back what they have given! So, is God a liar or are these scriptures metaphoric?

The Word of God cannot fail, and God is absolutely able to do what He promised in His Word. However, when it comes to giving and receiving, most Churches teach their members how to give, but not how to receive. Many believers think that once they give their financial seed, receiving financial miracles will be automatic.

Now, God can arrange for a stranger to give a believer a huge sum of money, or for a believer to find huge stacks of money under his bed.

However, this type of occurrence is the exception and not the rule. God prefers for His children to live in the supernatural and not in the miraculous.

Apostle Paul taught the Church in Philippi differently. He taught them about giving and receiving, and not just about giving.

> *"And as you Philippians know, in the early days of the gospel, when I left Macedonia, no church but you partnered with me in the matter of giving and receiving. For even while I was in Thessalonica, you provided for my needs again and again."* **Philippians 4:15 BSB**

Apostle Paul also told the believers that: *"… my God will supply all your needs according to His glorious riches in Christ Jesus."* **Philippians 4:19 [BLB]**

Just Like Farming

The process of sowing and reaping or planting and harvesting is usually used to explain giving and receiving. Therefore, considering the farming analogy, the process of giving is comparable to planting a crop. For instance, think about the work required to plant 100 hectares of tomatoes, how many seeds you require, what are the logistics involved, the labour requirement (usually one man on a tractor) etc. Receiving, on the other hand, is comparable to harvesting the same crop. Now think of harvesting 100 hectares of tomatoes. You will definitely need more than one person to get the job done on time; your logistics requirements will be way more complex than when you were sowing.

It is possible to store the seeds needed to plant 100 hectares of farmland in a few buckets in the kitchen. However, you cannot store the harvest of 100 hectares of tomatoes in a few buckets. You will require a proper storage facility and much more.

In other words, receiving is a totally different ball game from giving. In order to walk in the blessings of Abraham, you need to master both mysteries - sowing and reaping.

SOWING (=GIVING)

1.   Seed Preparation

Before you plant your seed, you need to think

about the quality of your seed. You cannot plant defective seed and expect a bumper harvest.

As a believer, when you give, is your seed a good seed or is it corrupted?

The scriptures say:

> *"Whoever sows sparingly will also reap sparingly, and whoever sows bountifully will also reap bountifully. Each one must give as he has decided in his heart, not reluctantly or under compulsion, for God loves a cheerful giver."*
>
> **2 Corinthians 9:6-7 ESV**

You cannot give the proceeds of corrupt practices and expect a bountiful harvest. The quality of your seed is important.

2. Site Preparation

Before you plant your seed, you must make sure you prepare the farm appropriately for planting. So, things like proper soil analysis, effective land clearing and ridging are important. You cannot plant apples on the beach and expect to get a fantastic harvest. That would be a wasted seed.

In the same vein, you must choose the ministry you give to carefully. Is the ministry genuinely engaged in advancing God's Kingdom or is it more focused on advancing the minister and his or her family?

This is very important if you truly want to experience God's returns from your giving. No farmer plants without doing proper due diligence on the land. So, as much as possible, do your research about the ministry you are giving to.

3.   Plant The Right Way

Sowing must be done correctly if you want the seed to grow and to yield good harvest. For example, if you put a seed too deep into the soil, it would die.

The scriptures say you must give your seed with rejoicing. If you give reluctantly, your giving is unacceptable to God. You are better off not giving at all than to give grudgingly or under compulsion

> *"Each one must give as he has decided in his heart, not reluctantly or under compulsion, for God loves a cheerful giver."* **2 Corinthians 9:7 ESV**

4.   Plant Management

After sowing your seed, it is important to manage the growth process. You need to water the seed, plant regularly, add things like manure or fertilizers at the right time, weed the plant to ensure it gets adequate air etc. All these are important to ensure you get a good harvest.

The same applies to a believers' giving. You cannot forget that you gave and expect to receive a harvest. A lot of believers give and forget they gave (well it's only $20 USD...).

> *"For surely there is an end; and thine expectation shall not be cut off."* **Proverbs 23:18 KJV**

Thanksgiving is also important to ensure an abundant harvest. As believers, we need to maintain an atmosphere of praise.

> *"Let the people praise thee, O God; let all the people praise thee. O let the nations be glad and sing for joy: for thou shalt judge the people righteously, and govern the nations upon earth. Selah*

Let the people praise thee, O God; let all the people praise thee.

Then shall the earth yield her increase; and God, even our own God, shall bless us.

God shall bless us; and all the ends of the earth shall fear him." **Psalm 67:3-7 KJV**

HARVESTING (=RECEIVING)

Harvesting is a very big deal. It is usually never incidental, and it requires proper planning. No farmer plants a farm and expects that by some miracle, the crop would harvest itself. When a farmer plants, he is already thinking about the harvest.

Harvest Preparation And Planning

Depending on the type of crop, a farmer must make sure a lot of things are in place to ensure a successful harvest. Let us take an example of strawberries. You cannot harvest strawberries with a tractor; you will need to employ a lot of labourers (depending on the size of the farm) to ensure the strawberries are harvested correctly.

Also, you cannot keep strawberries in a storage facility for too long. Hence, it IS important to have a buyer in place to take up the harvest.

How does this relate to receiving?

Well, a lot of believers are aware of the conditions that qualify a seed to yield good harvest; and God is ready to release to them a windows-of-heavens grade harvest, but unfortunately they do not have the platform to receive that type of return. As a result, the hundredfold return is withheld.

This is how it works in practice. A believer gives $1,000 monthly to a ministry that is actively engaged in the advancement of God's Kingdom. 100-fold of $1,000 is $100,000 (a hundred thousand dollars) monthly. Unfortunately, the believer only has a normal 9-to-5 job and earns $100,000 per annum. Now, because of the seeds sown, the believer is promoted and given a raise - he is now on $250,000 per annum. This income, $250,000 per annum is not 100-fold return of what was sown. It IS not even 30-fold return. But this is the best that child of God can receive because he does not have an appropriate platform to receive God's kind of harvest.

Imagine if this giver had his/her own business (as directed by the Holy Spirit), God could bless that venture in unimaginable ways such that the person that was once an employee could now be an employer of labour and like Isaac, could prosper and continue prospering until he becomes very prosperous. With men it is impossible, but for with God all things are possible (Mark 10:27 NKJV).

Having a Spirit-led platform to receive God's harvest is so important when we are engaged in the covenant practice of giving and receiving. Like the farmer that has to make sure all the systems are in place (storage, labour, offtake etc.) to ensure he/she does not lose or waste the harvest; every believer that desires to walk in the blessings of Abraham's must have a platform in place to receive the returns of their giving.

PERSONAL NOTES

_____

_____

_____

_____

_____

_____

_____

_____

_____

_____

_____

_____

_____

_____

_____

_____

_____

_____

_____

_____

_____

5

TITHING – A CLOSER LOOK

As highlighted earlier, the tithe is an eternal covenant put in place by God to usher in God's original blessing for mankind. As we have discovered in the Book of Genesis, God's will for mankind was that they will be Blessed.

> *"Then the Lord God took the man and put him in the garden of Eden to tend and keep it. And the Lord God commanded the man, saying, "of every tree of the garden you may freely eat; but of the tree of the knowledge of good and evil you shall not eat, for in the day that you eat of it you shall surely die."* **Genesis 2:15-17 NKJV**

The tithe did not originate in the old covenant. Therefore, it cannot be rendered irrelevant by the new covenant, as many people believe. In my opinion, the tithe is such an important key for the believer to live a supernatural and abundant life. Unfortunately, since it is not well understood by Christians, the benefits are not being realised; hence many have and are still agitating that it should no longer be practiced.

The Promises

To understand the benefits of tithing, let us look closely at what the Prophet Malachi had to say:

> *"Bring the full tithe into the storehouse, so that there may be food in My house. Test Me in this," says the LORD of Hosts. "*
>
> *See if I will not open the windows of heaven and pour out for you blessing without measure. I will rebuke the devourer for you, so that it will not destroy the fruits of your land, and the vine in your field will not fail to produce fruit," says the LORD of Hosts.*

"Then all the nations will call you blessed,
for you will be a land of delight," says the
LORD of Hosts." **Malachi 3:8-11 BSB**

There are not many places in the Bible where God says, "Test me with this," but He dared believers to test Him with the covenant of tithing.

1.   The Windows of Heaven's Blessing

God promised to open the windows of heaven and pour out blessings to us that are beyond measure when we pay our tithe. He does not open the windows of heaven all the time; the only other time He did so, the whole earth was flooded with rain.

"In the six hundredth year of Noah's life,
in the second month, on the seventeenth
day of the month, on that day all the
fountains of the great deep burst forth, and
the windows of the heavens were opened.
And rain fell upon the earth forty days and
forty nights." **Genesis 7:11-12 ESV**

2.   The Devourer shall be rebuked for you

Paul, writing to believers in Ephesus, said:

> *"For we do not wrestle against flesh and blood, but against principalities, against powers, against the rulers of the darkness of this age, against spiritual hosts of wickedness in the heavenly places."* **Ephesians 6:12 NKJV**

We are also admonished by the Apostle Peter in his first Epistle:

> *"Be sober, be vigilant; because your adversary the devil walks about like a roaring lion, seeking whom he may devour."* **1 Peter 5:8 NKJV**

Satan is the devourer. To ensure we excel against the forces of darkness, the scriptures says we should put on our whole armour and be prepared for battle.

> *"Put on the full armour of God, so that you will be able to stand firm against the*

schemes of the devil." **Ephesians 6:11 NASB**

Imagine if you never had to fight the devil again. Imagine the Lord dealing with the devil and his cohorts on your behalf. This is what you get when you pay your tithes; you and your family are protected al the time by the Almighty God Himself.

3.   Your Vine will not Fail to Produce

When you pay your tithes, God promised that your business will never fail. Whatever you embark upon, as led by the Holy Spirit, will succeed. There are so many principles taught globally on business success, and these body of knowledge is important. However, success is majorly spiritual. It is the blessing of the LORD that brings wealth, without painful toil for it (Proverbs 10:22 NIV).

The Covenant of the tithe guarantees that any believer can experience what Isaac experienced in Gerar - a business that would prosper and continue prospering until it becomes very prosperous.

4.   All Nations will call you Blessed

A believer that pays tithe is guaranteed a life of positive influence. As a tither, your friends, family, neighbours, and community will call you blessed. You will be a delight to them. This is God's promise to anyone that would honour God with their tithe. This is what Abraham, Isaac, and Jacob experienced in their walk with God.

Abraham was a force to be reckoned with in his community.

> *"Now when Abram heard that his brother was taken captive, he armed his three hundred and eighteen trained servants who were born in his own house, and went in pursuit as far as Dan. He divided his forces against them by night, and he and his servants attacked them and pursued them as far as Hobah, which is north of Damascus. So he brought back all the goods, and also brought back his brother Lot and his goods, as well as the women and the people.*
>
> *And the king of Sodom went out to meet*

him at the Valley of Shaveh (that is, the King's Valley), after his return from the defeat of Chedorlaomer and the kings who were with him." **Genesis 14:14-17 NKJV**

Isaac was acknowledged as blessed by his community.

"Then Abimelech came to him from Gerar with Ahuzzath, one of his friends, and Phichol the commander of his army. And Isaac said to them, "Why have you come to me, since you hate me and have sent me away from you?"

But they said, "We have certainly seen that the Lord is with you. So we said, 'Let there now be an oath between us, between you and us; and let us make a covenant with you, that you will do us no harm, since we have not touched you, and since we have done nothing to you but good and have sent you away in peace. You are now the blessed of the Lord.' "

So he made them a feast, and they ate and drank. Then they arose early in the

> *morning and swore an oath with one another; and Isaac sent them away, and they departed from him in peace."*
>
> **Genesis 26:26-31 NKJV**

And Jacob was considered indispensable to his in-laws. That is special.

> *"And it came to pass, when Rachel had borne Joseph, that Jacob said to Laban, "Send me away, that I may go to my own place and to my country. Give me my wives and my children for whom I have served you, and let me go; for you know my service which I have done for you."*
>
> *And Laban said to him, "Please stay, if I have found favour in your eyes, for I have learned by experience that the Lord has blessed me for your sake." Then he said, "Name me your wages, and I will give it."*
>
> **Genesis 30:25-28 NKJV**

Abraham, Isaac, and Jacob were tithers, and they all lived before the law. They were all exceptionally blessed. The scriptures say it only takes two or three witnesses to establish a truth.

> *"This will be the third time I am coming to you. "By the mouth of two or three witnesses every word shall be established."*
> **2 Corinthians 13:1 NKJV**

If believers are not experiencing the rewards of tithing like Abraham, Isaac, and Jacob did, it cannot be because tithing is no longer relevant or God is no longer faithful. It must be a lack of understanding of the mystery by believers in the Church today.

Let us explore the intricacies of this most powerful mystery instituted by the Lord Himself for the blessing of humanity, especially the Church.

Who is Your Melchizedek?

I have experienced a lot of wealth in my life, and I have God to thank for everything. However, a few years ago, I paid a large tithe of a business deal and was expecting an avalanche. To my shock, nothing happened. I was devastated and for months I could not stop inquiring from the Holy Spirit what went wrong. I had settled it in my heart ages ago that God is never wrong. If something is wrong, it must be me.

After a few months of persistent inquiry, early one morning, the Holy Spirit responded to me. He said, "Okay, you paid a lot of money as tithe from your last business deal, and you expected all the blessings as I promised. But wait a minute; did you pay the tithe to Melchizedek? Who exactly is your Melchizedek."

I was dumbfounded. The question caught me by surprise, and I did not know how to respond for days. But God who said, ask and it shall be given to you, seek and you shall find, knock and the door will be opened, is faithful (Matthew 6:6). I asked the Holy Spirit to explain to me what He meant by "who is your Melchizedek" and He responded. He said, your tithe is only acceptable when you give it to a ministry that's designated as a Melchizedek platform.

> *"Then Melchizedek king of Salem brought out bread and wine — since he was priest of God Most High and he blessed Abram and said:*
>
> *"Blessed be Abram by God Most High,*

Creator of heaven and earth, and blessed be God Most High, who has delivered your enemies into your hand."

Then Abram gave Melchizedek a tenth of everything. " **Genesis 14:18-20 BSB**

What is a Melchizedek Platform? it is:

1. A ministry that is genuinely involved in advancing the Kingdom of God, not one that is focused on enriching the minister, his family and his friends.

2. A Platform that manages the funds paid to it transparently and judiciously. Many ministries in our world today are not transparent at all; their accounts cannot be audited.

3. One that has auditable systems in place for managing its affairs.

4. One the prays for and blesses those who pay their tithe and offerings to the ministry. Melchizedek blessed Abraham after he paid his tithe. Lots of ministries do not even acknowledge receipt of the tithes, talk less of praying for their partners.

For example, the ministry of Eli, the high priest, was not a Melchizedek platform, and a lot of ministries in the Church today operates like the ministry of Eli. Paying tithes to these types of ministries is unacceptable to God and will not yield any divine rewards from the Lord as promised in Malachi 3:10-11.

> *"Now the sons of Eli were corrupt; they did not know the Lord. And the priests' custom with the people was that when any man offered a sacrifice, the priest's servant would come with a three-pronged fleshhook in his hand while the meat was boiling. Then he would thrust it into the pan, or kettle, or caldron, or pot; and the priest would take for himself all that the fleshhook brought up. So they did in Shiloh to all the Israelites who came there. Also, before they burned the fat, the priest's servant would come and say to the man who sacrificed, "Give meat for roasting to the priest, for he will not take boiled meat from you, but raw."*
>
> *And if the man said to him, "They should really burn the fat first; then you may take as much as your heart desires," he would*

then answer him, "No, but you must give it now; and if not, I will take it by force."
Therefore, the sin of the young men was very great before the Lord, for men abhorred the offering of the Lord.
1 Samuel 2:12-17 NKJV

As a young believer, I used to send my tithe to a ministry in the United States. I came across this ministry through the books written by the founder of the ministry. I was so excited about being a part of the work of this ministry - it literature distribution and TV broadcast (this was in the early nineties). Unfortunately, I did not see the promises I expected from my tithing.

It is important for me to stress at this juncture, God is not interested in anybody's money. There is no amount of money anyone can give that will get God excited. You must remember that the street of heaven is made with pure gold.

"The construction of its wall was of jasper; and the city was pure gold, like clear glass. The foundations of the wall of the city were adorned with all kinds of precious stones:

> *the first foundation was jasper, the second sapphire, the third chalcedony, the fourth emerald, the fifth sardonyx, the sixth sardius, the seventh chrysolite, the eighth beryl, the ninth topaz, the tenth chrysoprase, the eleventh jacinth, and the twelfth amethyst. The twelve gates were twelve pearls: each individual gate was of one pearl. And the street of the city was pure gold, like transparent glass."*
> **Revelation 21:18-21 NKJV**

God is interested in us being blessed. It is important, therefore, that we focus on the rewards of our obedience and if we do not see those rewards, we need to ask questions.

> *"But without faith it is impossible to please Him, for he who comes to God must believe that He is, and that He is a rewarder of those who diligently seek Him."* **Hebrews 11:6 NKJV**

By the second quarter of 1993, all sorts of horrifying revelations started to surface about the ministry: unopened prayer request letters were left in dump yards; the ostentatious lifestyle of the minister and his family became obvious, accusations of fraud and investigations, a failed libel case etc.

I was heartbroken because I regarded the ministry highly. However, I had the answer I was seeking answer as to why I had not received the rewards of my obedience. I promptly stopped sending any money to the ministry and asked the Holy Spirit to direct me to a genuine ministry that qualified as a Melchizedek platform.

What is the moral of my story? Every believer should carry out proper and due diligence enquiries on the ministry they support financially, and ensure they are led by the Holy Spirit to do so. Your money is the reward of your life. Do not waste it.

Just as a farmer is responsible for carrying out the appropriate research on the land he will be planting on, it is your responsibility as a believer, to make continual enquiries about integrity of the ministry you are paying your tithes and offerings into. Please note that continual due diligence enquires is an ongoing process. A ministry that is compliant today might not be a Melchizedek platform a few years down the line. The only thing that is certain and constant in life is change. The body of Christ is about people, and the obvious reality is that people change. Paul alluded to this in his letter to the believers in Corinth

> *"But I keep under my body, and bring it into subjection: lest that by any means, when I have preached to others, I myself should be a castaway."* **I Corinthians 9:27 KJV**

The Bread and the Wine

I love the word of God because it is all time relevant. While meditating on the scripture where Abraham paid his tithe to Melchizedek, I cannot help but wonder why Melchizedek brought bread and wine.

> *"Then Melchizedek king of Salem brought out bread and wine; he was the priest of God Most High. And he blessed him and said: "Blessed be Abram of God Most*

*High, Possessor of heaven and earth; And
blessed be God Most High, Who has
delivered your enemies into your hand."
And he gave him a tithe of all."*

Genesis 14:18-20 KJV

Why did he not bring rice, beans, lamb chops or
mashed potatoes? Why did he bring bread and
wine? What is the relevant of the bread and wine,
and its significance with the King of Salem's
encounter with Abraham? The bread and wine
depict the body and the blood of Jesus Christ shed
from Gethsemane, all the way to His crucifixion at
Golgotha.

*"As they were eating, Jesus took some
bread and blessed it. Then he broke it in
pieces and gave it to the disciples, saying,
"Take this and eat it, for this is my body."
And he took a cup of wine and gave thanks
to God for it. He gave it to them and said,
"Each of you drink from it, for this is my
blood, which confirms the covenant
between God and his people. It is poured
out as a sacrifice to forgive the sins of
many."* **Matthew 26:26-28 NLT**

Eternal Life

Melchizedek, the king of Salem, brought the elements of the communion thousands of years before the birth of Jesus. This is pretty deep and simply an eternal truth. They are not Old Testament practices or New Testament beliefs. They are eternal ordinances that transcend time. As I earlier mentioned, tithe is one of such ordinances. So also is the flesh and the blood.

Abraham honoured God and fulfilled his side of the covenant when he brought his tithe thus obeying God's instituted word to bless mankind. God, in other hand, had to fulfil His side of the bargain, and for that, He gave Abraham His flesh and His blood. Henceforth, Abraham began to walk in eternal life as it pertains to his finances.

Jesus said in John 6:53-54 [KJV]:

> *"Then Jesus said unto them, verily, verily, I say unto you, except ye eat the flesh of the Son of man, and drink his blood, ye have no life in you. Whoso eateth my flesh, and drinketh my blood, hath eternal life; and I will raise him up at the last day."*

What is Eternal Life?

"And this is life eternal, that they might know thee the only true God, and Jesus Christ, whom thou hast sent." **John 17:3 KJV**

The word *"know"* in John 17:3 is the greek word *"Ginosko"*. It means to understand, recognise, perceive and be acquainted with. In essence, it is only by taking the flesh of our Lord and drinking His blood, that a believer can experience this type of knowledge. This is the type of knowledge Daniel received to do exploits.

"Those who do wickedly against the covenant he shall corrupt with flattery; but the people who know their God shall be strong, and carry out great exploits." **Daniel 11:32 NKJV**

When Melchizedek gave Abraham the bread and the wine, the Lord released to Abraham the eternal life (or Ginosko) he needed to walk in the blessing. He received the grace to understand finances, recognize divine opportunities, perceive when God was leading him into a business breakthrough, and to become acquainted with God. What a blessing!

My hope is that you will understand the power of tithing as a believer, and that it is not an exercise to be carried out flippantly. It cannot and must not become a religious exercise. It is an opportunity for God to hand to you the keys to the knowledge (Ginosko) you need to walk in the blessing of Abraham, as well as the knowledge you need to be fruitful, and multiply, replenish the earth, subdue it and walk in dominion.

As a tithe paying believer, whenever you partake of the communion, expect God to hand over to you the keys of dominion over money. The same keys that Jesus had while He walked the face of the earth and gave him total mastery, and dominion over finances.

PERSONAL NOTES

_____

_____

_____

_____

_____

_____

_____

_____

_____

_____

_____

_____

_____

_____

_____

_____

_____

_____

_____

_____

_____

6

THE BLESSING IN ACTION

Jesus, as a God, owns all the resources in the world. Psalm 24:1 (NLT) says "The earth is the LORD's, and everything in it. The world and all its people belong to him."

However, as a man, He had to operate in the blessing of Abraham. While He walked the earth, Jesus was never stranded financially. He walked in divine favour financially, and operated in dominion over money and resources. You will never be stranded financially again; you will always find a way out of financial hardship in Jesus mighty name.

Let us explore instances in scripture where Jesus walked in the blessing of Abraham.

Jesus Supplies Wine Supernaturally

If you have ever had a party, you will understand the challenge Jesus faced at the wedding in Cana. Drinks are a major expense of a party comparable to the cost of food. In a wedding, the last thing you want to run out of is food and drinks. You could still have a bash with a crummy band and an unsightly venue but without enough food and drink, the party would be considered a flop.

> *"Jesus said to them, "Fill the waterpots with water." And they filled them up to the brim. And He said to them, "Draw some out now, and take it to the master of the feast." And they took it. When the master of the feast had tasted the water that was made wine, and did not know where it came from (but the servants who had drawn the water knew), the master of the feast called the bridegroom. And he said to him, "Every man at the beginning sets out the good wine, and when the guests have well drunk, then the inferior. You have kept the good wine until now."*
> **John 2:7-10 NKJV**

This is a type of money situations that causes believer to be panicky, become uneasy, fidgety, and fearful. But Jesus, knowing the power of the blessing of Abraham did not panic but had a solution. Remember, Jesus said, He only does what He sees the Father do. With respect to this matter, instead of panicking or getting flustered, He asked the Holy Spirit what should be done, and He did exactly what He was shown – awesome!

> *"So Jesus explained, "I tell you the truth, the Son can do nothing by himself. He does only what he sees the Father doing. Whatever the Father does, the Son also does."* **John 5:19 NLT**

When you operate in the Blessing, there is always a way of escape. It does not matter how scary that financial challenge looks, always remember it is common, God is faithful and there is a way of escape in the Holy Spirit.

> *"No temptation has overtaken you except such as is common to man; but God is faithful, who will not allow you to be*

tempted beyond what you are able, but with the temptation will also make the way of escape, that you may be able to bear it."
I Corinthians 10:13 NKJV

Jesus Feeds 5000 Men

Jesus had just finished a teaching and healing meeting in Bethsaida. He had a situation where he had to decide to feed all the attendees or tell them to leave, and sort themselves out. Many of us have been in this type of situation in our lives. We find ourselves having to decide what to do based on the availability of funds. We would love to go on that holiday, but we need to pay the bills. We really need to have a massage, but the mortgage is due. It would be really nice to help someone in dire need, but you cannot because you have to sort out your own issues too.

The Bible says, Jesus understands our challenges. In fact, He experienced similar challenges yet not one of those situations got him overwhelmed.

"For we do not have a high priest who is unable to empathize with our weaknesses, but we have one who has been tempted in every way, just as we are yet he did not sin." **Hebrews 4:15 NIV**

Jesus understood the power available to Him in the blessing of Abraham. He knew He had dominion over finances, and He could live the abundant life – He was abundant life.

Therefore, after the healing and teaching conference in Bethsaida, He decided to feed the hungry crowd rather than send them away.

"When the day began to wear away, the twelve came and said to Him, "Send the multitude away, that they may go into the surrounding towns and country, and lodge and get provisions; for we are in a deserted place here." But He said to them, "You give them something to eat." And they said, "We have no more than five loaves and two fish, unless we go and buy food for all these people." For there were about five thousand men.

Then He said to His disciples, "Make them sit down in groups of fifty." And they did so, and made them all sit down. Then He took the five loaves and the two fish, and looking up to heaven, He blessed and broke them, and gave them to the disciples to set before the multitude. So they all ate and were filled, and twelve baskets of the leftover fragments were taken up by them." **Luke 9:12-17 NKJV**

I have no idea how this miracle was done, or at what point the food multiplied and increased. But this revealed to me that was total dominion over resources, and the same is available to every believer that taps into the power of the Blessing.

There are two other instances I have come across, where God performed similar miracles (it is possible there are more). I believe as we meditate on these miracles, our finances will never run dry again in Jesus name.

The Widow of Zarephath

The first instance was when prophet Elijah had decreed to Ahab that there would be no rain or dew over Israel for a few years. Thereafter, He was directed by God to a brook by the Kerith ravine in Jordan where He was fed by ravens and drank from the brook. The brook dried up because there was no rain over the country. In essence, he was in a desperate situation.

When you are in a relationship with God, you will come to a deep understanding that with God, no situation can ever be hopeless. The key is our ability to access divine direction. The Lord instructed Elijah to leave Kerith ravine and move to Zarephath. God had a plan to ensure His servant would not be stranded throughout the period of drought.

> *"And the word of the LORD came unto him, saying, Arise, get thee to Zarephath, which belongeth to Zidon, and dwell there: behold, I have commanded a widow woman there to sustain thee. So he arose and went to Zarephath. And when he came to the gate of the city, behold, the widow woman was there gathering of sticks: and he called to her, and said, Fetch me, I pray thee, a little water in a vessel, that I may drink. And as she was going to*

fetch it, he called to her, and said, Bring me, I pray thee, a morsel of bread in thine hand. And she said, As the LORD thy God liveth, I have not a cake, but an handful of meal in a barrel, and a little oil in a cruse: and, behold, I am gathering two sticks, that I may go in and dress it for me and my son, that we may eat it, and die. And Elijah said unto her, Fear not; go and do as thou hast said: but make me thereof a little cake first, and bring it unto me, and after make for thee and for thy son.

For thus saith the LORD God of Israel, The barrel of meal shall not waste, neither shall the cruse of oil fail, until the day that the LORD sendeth rain upon the earth. And she went and did according to the saying of Elijah: and she, and he, and her house, did eat many days. And the barrel of meal wasted not, neither did the cruse of oil fail, according to the word of the LORD, which he spake by Elijah."
I Kings 17:8-16 KJV

Note, that the widow, only had a handful of meal in a barrel, and a little oil in a cruse. Her plan was to prepare the last meal for herself and her son to eat and die. But God had other plans. By divine intervention, the barrel of meal and the cruise of oil kept multiplying, and she never ran out until the drought was over.

It was God that miraculously caused the oil to keep flowing till all the vessels were filled. It is the same God that caused the barrel of meal not to waste, and the cruse of oil not to fail. This same God will miraculously multiply the funds in your hands, so you will never again be stranded financially in the Jesus mighty name.

Indeed, God is the same yesterday today and forever. He performed this miracle in the time of Elijah, and while Jesus walked on the earth. He is able to do the same today. Expect God to supernaturally multiply your resources to ensure you are never stranded again.

The Wife of the Son of the Prophet

Another instance was in the time of prophet Elisha. There was a son of the prophet who for some reason did not experience the financial provisions of the Blessing of Abraham while he lived. Being a son of the prophet indicates he was a lover of God. Unfortunately, when he died, his wife and sons were being hounded because of his debts.

This is so typical of many in our world today. isn't it? We are believers in God through our Lord Jesus Christ. Galatians 3:13 says Abraham's blessing belong to us, yet many believers are dead broke. I believe that this book will be the beginning of the turnaround for many believers in God through our Lord Jesus Christ.

Out of desperation, the widow of the son of the prophet sought out the prophet Elisha. Unlike her husband, she knew God was interested in her financial situation, and if anyone could help her unlock the door to financial abundance, it would have to be a genuine prophet of God.

She was full of humility and faith; and was obedient to God's instructions. God showed up for her and delivered her from financial stress supernaturally – indeed there is absolutely nothing God cannot do.

"A certain woman of the wives of the sons of the prophets cried out to Elisha, saying, "Your servant my husband is dead, and you know that your servant feared the Lord. And the creditor is coming to take my two sons to be his slaves."

So Elisha said to her, "What shall I do for you? Tell me, what do you have in the house?" And she said, "Your maidservant has nothing in the house but a jar of oil."

Then he said, "Go, borrow vessels from everywhere, from all your neighbours — empty vessels; do not gather just a few. And when you have come in, you shall shut the door behind you and your sons; then pour it into all those vessels and set aside the full ones."

So she went from him and shut the door behind her and her sons, who brought the vessels to her; and she poured it out. Now it came to pass, when the vessels were full, that she said to her son, "Bring me another vessel."

And he said to her, "There is not another vessel." So the oil ceased. Then she came and told the man of God. And he said,

> *"Go, sell the oil and pay your debt; and you and your sons live on the rest."*
> **I Kings 4:1-7 NKJV**

Jesus Pays Taxes Miraculously

In Capernaum, Jesus and Peter were confronted with an unexpected tax bill, which is a very serious matter. Jesus was facing a situation that could cause Him a lot of shame and ridicule. But as usual, He understood the power of the blessing and looked for the answer in the Holy Spirit.

> *"And when they were come to Capernaum, they that received tribute money came to Peter, and said, Doth not your master pay tribute? He saith, Yes. And when he was come into the house, Jesus prevented him, saying, What thinkest thou, Simon? Of whom do the kings of the earth take custom or tribute? Of their own children, or of strangers? Peter saith unto him, of strangers. Jesus saith unto him, Then are the children free."* **Matthew 17:24-26 KJV**

Jesus refused to panic. He knew the Holy Spirit knows all things and would show Him what to do.

> *"Howbeit when he, the Spirit of truth, is come, he will guide you into all truth: for he shall not speak of himself; but whatsoever he shall hear, that shall he speak: and he will shew you things to come."* **John 16:13 KJV**

> *"But the anointing which ye have received of him abideth in you, and ye need not that any man teach you: but as the same anointing teacheth you of all things, and is truth, and is no lie, and even as it hath taught you, ye shall abide in him."* **I John 2:27 KJV**

He instructed Peter to go fishing, and that Peter would find the funds to settle their tax bill in the mouth of the first fish he catches – what a miracle working God.

> *"Notwithstanding, lest we should offend them, go thou to the sea, and cast an hook,*

*and take up the fish that first cometh up;
and when thou hast opened his mouth,
thou shalt find a piece of money: that take,
and give unto them for me and thee."*

Matthew 17:27 KJV

You do not have to be afraid of any unexpected bills ever again. Through Jesus Christ, we are free from the curse of the law; situations and circumstances can no longer dominate us. We have dominion. We no longer have to live a subdued life, but instead, we should begin to walk in the blessing of Abraham just like Jesus did.

PERSONAL NOTES

_____

_____

_____

_____

_____

_____

_____

_____

_____

_____

_____

_____

_____

_____

_____

_____

_____

_____

_____

_____

_____

_____

_____

_____

_____

_____

_____

_____

_____

_____

_____

_____

_____

_____

_____

_____

_____

_____

_____

_____

_____

_____

_____

_____

_____

_____

_____

7

CONFESSIONS FOR FINANCIAL VICTORY

God wants to prosper His people always. God's will is to always prosper His people. He will never forget you nor forsake you. When it seems like there is nothing you can do, speak faith, speak victory. Begin today with these confessions for financial victory and declare by faith.

1.   Abraham's BLESSING belongs to me. Abundance and prosperity are God's will for my life, so I declare myself debt free in Jesus name. I declare my mortgage, car loans and debts are paid off. God's favour and BLESSING are active, and are operating in every area of my life (Galatians 3:14-29; Romans 13:8; Psalm 5:12).

2.   Everything I do prospers and succeeds. The wisdom of God helps me to make sound financial decisions. I am blessed and highly favoured among men (Deuteronomy 30:9; Psalm 1:3).

3.   My God supplies all my needs according to His riches in glory. He is Jehovah Jireh—my Provider. My job is not my source. My credit cards and my relatives are not my source. God is my only source of supply, and I trust in Him (Philippians 4:19).

4.   I refuse to worry about my financial situation. I will not fall into the temptation to fear or have anxiety. I cast my cares over onto the Lord. If He takes care of the birds and flowers, He will certainly take care of me (Matthew 6:25-34).

5.   I am a faithful tithe paying believer, and because I pay my tithe, my finances are protected from the devourer. Right now, I rebuke the devourer in the name of Jesus. I command you to release my finances now and flee. I plead the blood of Jesus over my money and my possessions. No

weapon formed against me, my family or my finances will prosper in Jesus' name (Malachi 3:10-11; Luke 18:12; Isaiah 54:17).

6.   I seek first the kingdom of God, therefore, everything I need will be added to me. The Lord takes pleasure in my prosperity, so I declare that I am prosperous in Jesus name. I have more than enough, I am blessed to be a blessing. I am a giver, and I receive a hundredfold return in Jesus' name (Matthew 6:33; Psalm 35:27; Mark 10:30).

7.   I walk in the spirit of self-control with my finances. I will not be tempted to overspend or lust after material possessions. I am a faithful steward of the finances God has blessed me with, and I will not go into debt from this day forward. I choose to live by faith (Galatians 5:16; Psalm 119:66; Hebrews 10:38).

8.   I delight myself in the Lord, and He gives me the desires of my heart (Psalm 37:4).

9.   I refuse to fear or be shaken by financial trials. I have the peace of God operating in my life,

and I know God has a plan for me to experience financial victory in my life. I cast every situation over onto my God. He is my Provider, my Deliverer, and my Strong Tower. I will wait patiently in faith for the direction of the Holy Spirit. I am victorious in my finances. (Isaiah 43:19; John 14:1; John 14:27; Hebrews 13:5; 2 Corinthians 2:14).

Keep believing and speaking these daily confessions for financial victory, and you will see the glory of the Lord in your finances. No matter how troubling your situation, God can and will turn it around. He will make a way where there seems to be no way. Trust in Him, keep the faith, and stand in your financial victory.

PRAYER OF SALVATION

If you do not know Jesus as your Saviour and Lord, simply pray the following prayer in faith, and Jesus will be your Lord.

Heavenly Father, I come to You in the name of Jesus. Your word says, "Whosoever shall call on the name of the Lord shall be saved" (Acts 2:21). I am calling on You now. I pray and ask Jesus to come into my heart and be the Lord over my life according to Romans 10:9-10: "If thou shalt confess with thy mouth the Lord Jesus, and shalt believe in thine heart that God has raised him from the dead, thou shalt be saved. For with the heart man believeth unto righteousness; and with the mouth confession is made unto salvation." Now I confess that Jesus is Lord, and I believe in my heart that God raised Him from the dead.

I am now reborn. I am a Christian—a child of the Almighty God. I am saved! You also said in

Your word, "If ye then being evil, know how to give good gifts unto your children: how much more shall your heavenly Father give the Holy Spirit to them that ask him?" (Luke 11:13). I am also asking You to fill me with the Holy Spirit. Holy Spirit, rise up within me as I praise God. I fully expect to speak with other tongues as You give me the utterance (Acts 2:4) in Jesus name. Amen.